Each from the Heart:
Special Letters Just For You

Maria Manuela Pinto

www.mariamanuelapinto.com
facebook.com/MariaManuelaPintoAuthor
twitter.com/MariaManuelaPi4

Publisher: Mariangelikuss

Mariangelikuss

DEDICATION

This lovely book, *Each from the Heart: Special Letters Just For You*, is dedicated to those who at some moment in their lives wanted to communicate with their loved ones and didn't know how to start – especially how to touch their hearts without hurting their feelings.

CONTENTS

ACKNOWLEDGMENTS

I give thanks to my family for the unconditional love and support that they gave me while I wrote this wonderful book. Thank you to each and every one of you. To my husband and three children with love: may God bless you today and always.

To My Mother

I can see her with a lost, tired gaze, as if she wanted to bring back her memories of her youth.

Many memories appear in her mind, and she hasn't spoken a single word of them to me, but it's almost as if she told me much of her life through her expression.

In that stillness I felt her cry, laugh, sing, and dance; I experienced her disappointments, her woes and her joys, and all the sentiments and remembrances that filled her life with love.

But what I most admired about her was her endless faith and sense of humor. She always smiled even when there was misfortune and always gave a word of hope whenever there was worry.

For these things and many more, I also, in silence, want to say: "I love you, Mother." Thank you for all or what little you have given me. For me it's been your unconditional love, your wisdom, and your advice.

You've always worried about us all, your family. I don't want to forget to mention the skills you have for cooking and baking sweets. You always put so much passion into it, that your confections were to die for.

May God bless you today and forever.

****

To My Father

I remember you as if I had seen you yesterday; every day of my life, to be more precise. You'll always be with me.

You welcomed me to this marvelous world with a grand smile, you took me into your arms and couldn't believe that you had become a father!

You helped me take my first steps; you did the same with my first words. You even bought me my first bicycle, and I remember all the times I fell off of it and you would say:
"If you fall, you get back up. That way you'll learn faster."

How right you were.

You worked intensely so that I could have everything I needed. We grew up together, you with your necessities and me with mine.

Discovering different stages of our lives.

When I didn't understand, you made it so that I could. You made me realize that every person is different, with their own defects and virtues, and that to err is human but so is to forgive.

There has always been communication between us. I felt respect for you, and you always had a loving word for me.

How important communication can be.

You showed me the value of things, that everything we aim for could be reached with strength and resolve.

Now I have the capacity to do everything within my reach in order to come out on top, follow through with my goals, make my dreams reality, and most importantly, give love.

I know how to face the problems of daily life, and when I've fallen I've gotten up, just like when I learned to ride my first bicycle.

Thank you for your teachings, which I'll never forget.
On the contrary, I've always kept them close, and you don't know how
much they've been of help to me.

I know you'll read this letter, where you'll find yourself and you'll
become delighted.

You'll be in my heart, today and always.

****

Addicted To You

I need you in the morning,
when the sun rises, and we'd have breakfast like every other day.
I'd ask you, "How did you sleep, my love?" and we'd tell of our dreams
and nightmares.
And why not love each other a little bit more?

I need you in the afternoon.
We'd have our lunch together, our favorite meal, and you'd tell me your
plans, your problems, your delights and your sorrows.
In the end, we'd talk a little about everything, and when we're through
we'll love each other just a little bit more.

I need you at night,
when the sun sets and the moon appears, for us to be lovers, friends,
accomplices, and something more.

As you can see, I need you all the hours of the day,
every month of the year.
"Have I become addicted to you?"

If I love you like this, the way that I do - with that uncontrollable passion
and love that you awaken in me each second, each minute, each day - I
could call it addiction.

So I am entirely addicted to you, out of love.

****

MARIA MANUELA PINTO

<u>Goodbye, Love of Mine</u>

If only you heard what I murmur in your ear, you'd realize how vast the love that I hold for you is.

*A love that's pure, unpolluted; never a negative thought.
A devotion that's complete; and always possessing the most intense desires for you.*

I'll continue coming here, like every night, dressed in white like an angelic bride. I'll kiss and contemplate you the way I always do.

*If only you paid more attention to me, you'd realize that I always adore you in silence. Sleep, my love, sleep peacefully.
I know one day you'll hear me say:*

"Goodbye, love of mine."

It may be too late to regain lost time.

I'll come tomorrow, like every night, to take care of your dreams, give you my love and wish you good night, until the time to part comes, and I know I'll be missed.

Sleep, love of mine, and when you can't feel me near, don't worry, for I will not leave you alone; if you wish it and ask it of me, I will come for you, for us to love in a special place that I have in the heavens for you.

Goodbye, love of mine.

****

Beloved

I didn't understand why each time I got close to John, he didn't look at me. I even got to thinking he no longer loved me.

My days and nights were spent like this, until I noticed that I had passed on and was now a spirit.
At first I was very unhappy; so much, in fact, that I could not stop crying for days. I'd say that it must have been months of misery.

But the best thing that was happening to me was that I could now see everything that went on around John, and I could console him and give him the will to live when I saw him awfully depressed.

He, my beloved, had good and bad days.
How else could it have been? I had left his side. It had been many years that we lived together.
By means of this letter, beloved John, I want to tell you many things.

I want to say that I find myself doing well.
The physical pains have left me for good, I see you almost everyday, I'm always with you, and I enjoy your moments of happiness and give you consolation in your moments of sadness.

Being here is not for worse, but for better.
There is much peace and most of all, I am content.
From here I can keep loving you and looking after you.

Enjoy what you have with you now; your children and grandchildren, which are of limitless value.

I miss you all and I'll never stop loving you.
It was I who had to pass on first, but I accept my destiny.

My beloved, I always will be with you.

****

Agony of Love

I am anxious to have you here with me.
How you warm my cold nights, how you kiss me, the way only you can.

How your gentle hands caress my body, admiring it with your sweet,
angelic look, and undressing not only my body but my soul as well.
By doing so you will realize that I belong to you completely.

I await you with desperation, but the minutes feel like the longest hours.
I yearn for you with all of my heart. What kind of attraction do you hold?

Just by thinking of you, my heart becomes agitated and my body grows
restless to have you. My love, do not take any longer, for this wait is
already an agony of love.

I am dying of love for you, ever since I first beheld you, and I fell
insanely in love with you. You are an angel on earth; sweet, sensual,
with a melodious voice which is music to my ears.

You are made of flesh and bone but to me you are a celestial being.

Do not take any longer, as my heart will start to melt and you might find
crystallized droplets; tears of my crying for you.

I did not know, until I met you, that the agony of love existed.

****

Friendship

You can't find it in any place. It's it that finds you.

Many times it comes and goes, but when it stays with us everything changes, because Friendship is unconditional.
It talks to you, listens to you, understands you, and helps you without asking for anything in return.

Friendship doesn't quantify its sentiments, it gives them all to you.

Friendship is translucent like the clear waters of a river.

Friendship is delicate like the petal of a rose.

When you call it, it's the first to come and keep you company, give you support, and give you guidance without caring about anything else. It needs to be there with you, in good times and bad.

Friendship, you are free like a bird; fly and make your nest where you're given warmth and love.

But when Friendship is dishonored, it leaves never to return, leaving an empty space that you don't know how to fill.

Sadness consumes you and you feel lonely, very lonely.

Why did Friendship leave?

It left because it didn't receive the same feelings it gave. It felt disgraced and departed from your side.

Friendship is fabulous, so don't let it go.

If you're lucky to find it in your path, grab a hold of it tightly and with all of your heart.

Because if it came to you, it found an interest in you - as a friend.

Friendship has no age.
It has no color or religion. It doesn't have a political view, it doesn't discriminate, it's quiet and loving, it doesn't judge, nor does it possess prejudices.

Friendship has many qualities and almost no defects.

Friendship will give you real love.

It'll value your human worth. It is priceless, like when you receive a precious gift and on its packaging it says:

"One hundred percent legitimate."

Thank you, Friendship, for coming to me. I am fortunate to have you.

****

Same Sex Love

A friend of mine wrote me a letter; I replied with this:

If a man loves another man, or if a woman loves another woman,
let them be happy. Falling in love with someone of the same sex is not
bad, it's love, and love is something the whole world needs.

I don't see anything absurd about it,
and neither is it something to be surprised about.
They want to live together, share their lives with each other, their ideals,
their thrills and their sorrows like every human being.
They have every right to be happy, and they've done no one any harm.

On the contrary, give them your unconditional support, which is real
love. Criticizing them and going against the love that they have for one
another will only bring negativity and will make both your life and theirs
very unhappy. Enough of that!

Time to create, not destroy! The world is very large and everybody,
absolutely everybody inhabits it.
For all the homosexual couples who decided to be together;

my best wishes and hopes that you start a life full of love.
We're human beings, divine creatures; we're the children of God,
so we should give and receive love as well as learn to live with
and respect one another.

****

Anguish

What anguish I feel, knowing that you will no longer come and I won't see you anymore.

Is it because you've forgotten about me and don't need me anymore?

Today is our anniversary and you're not here with me to celebrate and toast to our love.

I feel anguish in my heart.
It seems like it will break and I won't be able to repair it.

Such anguish I feel within my soul; the strongest pain I've felt for love, because I've lost you and there won't be anything or anyone that can give me solace.

Even my tears have dried up from so much weeping.

But the most anguish I get is from knowing that I'll never love anyone as much as you.

****

Rainbow

If you observe the sky, very soon will you see the rainbow appear.

The seven colors of love, peace, happiness, hope, friendship, joy, strength, etc. It contains many more emotions; as many as it can hold.

The color yellow - good luck.
We all need it, and how!

The color red - power.
Natural strength that pushes you to attain all that you desire.

The color indigo - peace.
What the world is in desperate need of.

The color green - hope.
What should never be lost.

The color blue - relaxation and meditation.
It helps you connect with your inner you.

The color violet - love.
The biggest sentiment which exists in the universe.

The color orange - joy and celebration.
It should always be with us.

God created it for each and every one of us, so we could enjoy the spectacle and dream of its colors. Close your eyes and travel to where your senses and emotions take you.

When the rainbow appears, that is your opportunity to open your heart and your conscience.

It brings love, it brings emotions so profound that all the creatures of the planet should practice them daily.

****

Aroma of Love

I sit at the edge of a river, closely watching its mesmerizing ripples,
where for a few minutes I lose myself in its crystalline waters.

I can sense a sweet aroma, something like dried fruits with cinnamon;
perhaps fresh strawberries just harvested from the orchard, or maybe
fresh honey, I don't know.

But the aroma can be smelt with much more intensity now.

I close my eyes and start to imagine beautiful things.
Memories of my childhood, adolescence, and every phase of my life pass
through my mind.

Between the sweet scent and the sound of the rippling water, I feel that
they take me to wherever my conscience wants to go.

After five minutes, I can see it coming toward me; it can only be him!
The aroma of love.

That love, for which I have waited for so long and at last I can feel.
So now I must say that love has an aroma of cinnamon, fresh fruits,
sugar and honey!

****

You Looked Different Yesterday

*You seem changed, since the last night we saw each other. I ask myself,
"Our honeymoon didn't last very long, did it?"*

*I want to think that this is just a bad dream, because that's all it could
ever be after having many moments filled with love from living together.*

*Moments of joy, always smiling about everything.
Life was like a carousel for us, going around and around and we saw it
upside-down and right-side up.
We were always together and very much in love.*

You looked different yesterday.

*Staring at the rays of sunlight so breathtaking and those nights when the
moon was full in a sky illuminated by the stars, but also by our love.*

*I remember when we ate fresh cherries, since I always loved to collect
the seeds, and I said to you, "I will keep these and plant them in my
garden so that we may have cherries every day of the year."*

You looked different yesterday.

*I'll never forget when we decided to go to the blue forest.
That's what they called it, but it wasn't blue. I was so ingenuous that I
began to think that there might exist a blue forest.*

*I remember when I made a basket filled with the most scrumptious
turnovers. I wasn't an expert cook, but I put a lot of creativity into
baking those pastries and, needless to say, other sweets.
They were all delectable!*

*When you ate them, you had said, "So sweet - like you."
You were always romantic and very much in love.*

*You looked different yesterday;
so different, in fact, that I couldn't recognize you.*

You aren't the same man with whom I spent long nights of love.
You aren't the same man with whom I shared my bed and with whom I
woke up every morning.

With eyes closed, betting all I had, not caring about anything else, I
offered myself to you, totally nude of both body and soul the way I came
into this world. That's how I wanted you and that's how I still do.

Did something change today?
Perhaps I should not ask;
perhaps I should stay with those memories.

The only thing I know is that I adore you very much, as you do I.
If something happened I don't want to know about it anymore.
I will stay with your caresses, your kisses, your way of loving so
profound. It's what I keep close to my body and my heart.

What we lived with was so beautiful and I will keep it as such within the
most intimate part of my being.

****

Help Yourself First

To start a new day we should make the effort of meeting our goals, not
leave them for tomorrow because these are part of our lives.

When human beings see their projects finished, they feel complete and
this, therefore, makes them happy.

Let's make it so that our lives change for the better, a little bit each day.
Don't forget about yourselves, because you're the main protagonists of
your existence.

Our plans, objectives, resolutions, dreams: we should make these reality
otherwise we'll be incomplete and unhappy.

Our lives would be so much better if we started with ourselves,
so in that way we would be much more happy and we would give
happiness to others.

You can't be recommended to eat a chicken fillet,
if you've never tried it before.

We love to give advice and suggestions,
many times without having tried them ourselves.

Let's put this old saying to use:

"Give to receive."

In order to give, first we must learn to receive.

****

<u>*Baby*</u>

God has sent you the best gift of all.

The most glorious of its kind,

The most sweet and heavenly;

so small it appears,

who is to say its soul is as big as infinity?

The day it was born, your hearts lit up.

How couldn't it have been that way?

Upon awakening, it gives you the light to brighten your days.

It gives you the serenity to calm your anxieties.

It gives you so much love, that by holding your hands you will learn,

from it as it will learn from you, its own parents.

God has sent you the best gift of all, called

"baby."

****

Espresso

If only you'd give me a sign that you're here with me.
What I wouldn't do for another minute with you.
To be able to tell you so many things that I haven't yet.

For example; the great love I've always had for you, and perhaps I've
not told it to you in the way you would have wanted to hear.
Even though I showed it to you, saying it is much more meaningful.

Give me a sign. I'll do everything in my power to be with you, feel you
close to me, embrace you tightly and tell you that I love you with all of
my heart and that I still do.

Can you imagine us going back to the places we loved?
To sightsee and talk about the things we usually did and the many
dreams we shared.

Give me a tiny sign and everything will change forever.
I'll recognize you immediately. How couldn't I?
I know you so well, my senses will point you out to me.

I'm making the espresso that you were so fond of.
Remember how you used to drink it?
Little by little, sip by sip, oh how you relished it.

For whom and why am I doing this?
Only for you.

Who will I drink this with?
Only with you.

Why, how foolish I've been! You've already given me a sign!

It's the espresso, your favorite!

****

Letter to a Priest

You will come tonight like almost every night.
I wait for you impatiently like a girl in love for the first time, when she
waits for her boyfriend behind her parents' backs without giving the
consequences of this moment of love any thought.

I know that I'm in some way sinning, you being a priest and me a free
woman who passionately loves you.
You have invaded my body, soul, and heart.

I never thought I'd fall in love with a priest, but your pure soul, your
sincere look, your sensual smile, your caresses and your wisdom made
me fall in love with you.

You're genuine, you speak with the truth and I believe that the time
has come for you to face this truth: that you love a woman.

For the time being I share you with the church; I know you love us
both. But in the end, isn't it love that you teach? Why can't we be happy?
We're only human beings with emotions.

I can't wait to see you, without that black uniform that you wear,
always clean and well pressed; to look into your eyes of blue like the
ocean, and to love each other until dawn.

Just by thinking of having you with me tonight gives me goose bumps.
I never thought a priest could love woman with so much passion,
sensuality and tenderness. Who taught you to love like that? You have so
many lovely qualities and emotions that I couldn't help falling in love.

There are times when we don't need to let our bodies unite in
passion; our hearts are already united with love.

A love that grows with each day.

****

<u>Today</u>

I realize that I've grown, that I've changed for the better.
I'll keep doing so because we're human beings with ambitions and
dreams, and because we want to be better,
and continue to grow each day.

A minute is worth more than that.
You can win or lose, but who cares about competition?
I think what's really important to us is to be happy!

I'm not interested in criticisms. However, I can listen to advice.
There's always something new to discover and learn.

Today,
I love myself more.
I've understood that life is short and I need to take advantage,
of every second.
Living life to the fullest with all of its good and bad moments,
is all I have and I should take care of that.

Today,
I see everything differently.
Everything that I learned I will put into practice.
I'm sure that the way I'm happy now,
I'll give the same happiness to others.

In the end, it's not only me who will be grateful, but God will be as
well, from seeing that the human beings with consciences he put on this
marvelous earth have been destined to be happy.

Because of this they will give love and receive it as well.

****

Letter to My Friends

I don't want a single day to go by without telling you that it was wonderful seeing you again.

It seems like yesterday that we had just gotten out of school, and now that we've found each other after all these years and I've seen you all again, I realize that not much has changed about you, and whatever has, has been for the better.

We've stayed with that joy from when we were schoolmates.

I noticed your souls were clean and your hearts open to love - unconditional and real love.

I'm writing this letter with all of my sincere love for you. How good it is to have you and know that if I need you, you'll be there. What pleasant emotions you express after so many years; you're all the same as before.

You all have big hearts and can give love, confidence, honesty, loyalty- I could keep going, but I won't, since you also have your defects. If you didn't, you wouldn't be as genuine as you are.

Even though we can't see each other as often as we'd like, I know that our hearts will stay unified through the most lovely memories of our youth.

****

I Waited For You For So Long

I waited for you for so very long, that upon waking up in the morning,
I felt your presence.
I prepared the coffee - your favorite blend - and I got ready the blue suit
that you liked so much and left it hung in the wardrobe.

I cooked your favorite dish and set the table impeccably with fresh
flowers, a white tablecloth and silverware.
We were having a celebration! It was the least I could do.

I waited for you for so long that night came quickly.
It was the time for sleep but I knew you were coming, you couldn't be
missing; we had a very special engagement.
I was dressed in black, your favorite color.

I felt you arrive. I could recognize you instantly, as well as that
fragrance you always wore. How could I forget it?
You kissed me and said, "Darling, I'm here at last."

How delightful to see him! I was so happy, my heart fluttered and my
senses vibrated with emotion.
My body couldn't contain the desire I had to hug him,
kiss him, and love him.

The wait had been so long that I thought I couldn't withstand it - the
anxiety consumed me. But love knows how to wait.

That night we loved, many times over, with passion, desire, and
intensity. I've waited for you for so, so long that the wait had turned into
a fantasy of love.

****

The Ocean

We met on a beautiful beach with sands of white, like your soul; with
transparent waters and penetrating waves, like your eyes; with a
brilliantly shining sun, the way only you could be.

What lovely days we spent on that beach, needless to say the nights
we had as well, but I should describe them for their nocturnal beauty.

The only light illuminating that night of love was the gleam of the
moon, where the stars shoved one another in order to be seen in the sky,
and so they could serve as witnesses of the passion and love
we held for each other.

There was nothing more clear and pure than the love we gave each
other on that special night. It's something I will never erase from my
mind, much less my heart.

The surf of the ocean and its calming waves brought out in us the
need to love, losing track of time.

The dawn of each morning was beautiful.
It welcomed us to a new day. The nights were brightened by the stars,
who drew our entwined bodies on the white sand.

I watched the ocean and asked it in silence,
"What are you hiding between those waves? How many encounters of
love have your profound, crystalline waters observed?"

I'm sure that, like this love, there have been no others.
I have loved it so much that I came back to tell you about it, because you
are the only witness to what we lived with, he and I.
Only you could understand me, my friend, the ocean.

The ocean brought us together but it also drove us apart.
It gave us our love but it also took it back from us.
Despite that, the ocean will continue to be our greatest ally
and our closest friend.

****

Faith

It's very dark here and I can't see the light anywhere.
I'm lost, but how can that be if I've followed your steps so carefully?

So much so, that I haven't even noticed that you aren't in front of me
anymore, leading me on and showing me the path to take.

"Where are you? Why have you gone so quickly and left me alone?
Is it because you don't want to help me cross this long road?"

I don't understand. You've told me time and time again that you'd
always be with me, and now when I need you most I can't find you.

My soul is beginning to grow anxious, I'm confused;
I think I'll lose myself if you don't appear.

I ask of you to come, I ask you to not leave me unprotected.
I need you here with me.
I nearly don't have the strength to continue.
I'm struggling to endure it all.

"I always have been with you, very close to you, accompanying you
on this long journey that you've been made to go on.
I have never abandoned you, I never would.
Your little faith made you see something that wasn't there.

I only ask you to have faith."

****

Gypsy

My eyes water just by thinking of you. I've loved you for so long that I couldn't live without you. I want you to know that you're a part of me.

Gypsy of my heart!

When I hear the flamenco I get goose bumps all over. I can almost see you dancing with those movements that will drive anyone mad.

My heart pounds without any sign of it slowing down, thinking of your youthful face and those castanets that you never stop playing.

You're full of life, like a spinning top; those we used to play with on the streets of our neighborhood. A spinning top that keeps on spinning.

What do you have that's so special, that my soul won't stop crying out of joy? Only by thinking that I might see you tonight, night turns into day for me.

Gypsy, you know full well that I couldn't live without your high heels and the colorful clothing that you always wear.

Last night I thought, "Where could my friend, the gypsy, be? Where did she run off to?"

Don't break my heart. You know full well that I feel you deep inside me, your gypsy blood that flows through your veins and mine as well.

You've accompanied me for so very long, don't leave now. It wouldn't be fair for either of us. Gypsy, my friend, keep dancing and clicking those heels; don't ever give up on it, as you do it through your heart!

You've always been unconditional, always with me. We even danced together, remember?

You taught me how to click heels as well, and I'm not so bad at it.

I can already feel your happiness - you're close - your smile, those castanets that you never stop playing, and your aroma of lavender, the most important; the lavender that you use to bewitch.

To bewitch all those that get close to you.
You are so special, that wherever you go, you leave love and contentment.

You were always my closest friend.
You know how to keep my most private thoughts well hidden.
You're trustworthy and loyal.

Gypsy of my heart!

If I cry, you comfort me. If I laugh, you laugh with me.
You're always there with me and for me.

There! I hear the clicks of your heels! You're here!

What a lovely dress you're wearing today! And your shoes!

How beautiful you've made yourself, how well the color red suits you.

The color of love and passion. Could it be that you're in love?

Gypsy of my heart!

****

Thank You, My God

I don't know how to express the joy in my heart.
This happiness is so grand that it overwhelms my soul.
I want to tell you so many things, I don't even know where to begin, but I
will start by giving thanks for the many splendid things,
I have been born with.

Qualities and defects like all human beings. I'm not eminent in
anything but I am a divine being in everything, the way you made me.

Here are our senses, for without them we'd be nothing:
sight, taste, hearing, touch, smell,
and not to mention our sixth sense, intuition.

All we need to do is open our minds, hearts, and souls in order to
better understand the being we carry within; one that is amazing.
Let's be aware of what we are.

The more I discovered it, the more surprised I was at the capacity of
love that we have in our hearts and with our extraordinary minds.

So, why waste time with negative thoughts
when we can be positive in everything that we do?
Thank you, my God, for giving us the capacity to reason.

I only ask you to think about what I've just told you.
You will realize that there are many instances when we waste time with
thoughts that damage the soul and disturb the heart.

****

Guardian

I know that it cares for me,
it looks after me at night and also during the day.

I know that it hears me, my joys and my sorrows.

I know that it feels me, when I'm uncomfortable and at peace.

I know that it watches me and does not neglect me.

I hear it say, "With you I will stay; I will not leave.

I'm your guardian, of whom you'll never wonder,

'Where are you?'

Wherever you want to be, I'll be there too."

****

<u>Spirit Guide</u>

There are many things I have learned these past days.
So many new and wonderful things have happened to me that I find them
hard to explain.

I felt you arrive, you spoke to me and I listened with close attention.
You appeared like light, a shining, beautiful light full of peace; that's
what I felt on that angelic night.
It was so special that my life changed completely.

Thank you for coming. I can't live without you now,
you're my day and my night.

You take care of me, you protect me, you guide my steps so I won't
trip; you light my way so I can't get lost, and most importantly, you love
me. I feel you so close to me.

Just by thinking of how we met I get chills, but those are out of
happiness, because I know you're here.

I'll never forget your first words to me:
"We're close now. We'll be communicating now."
That celestial voice amazed me so much that from then on we united to
never separate, for all eternity.

You are my spirit guide.

****

Flower Garden

Its aromas are so pleasing and its colors are so pretty that all and every one of its flowers enchant me.

Poppies, roses, lilies, violets, gardenias; there are so many that I can't remember the names of them all.

But I do remember those that you gave me on that summer afternoon, the best time of the year, not only because I met you but also because I fell in love with you.

Such lovely flowers you presented to me, and you said:

"A posy of splendid flowers for a lovely lady, where I can easily see the grandeur of your heart.

I made no mistake in choosing you as the most beautiful of all. You are like these flowers, fresh and delicate, with the sensual aroma of a divine woman, one who is charming and fragile, much like the roses.

I fell madly in love with you, but it's worth it for a woman like you. It's like finding a flower garden in the middle of the road; colorful, fresh, and sensual, just like you."

I went home and placed the flowers in a vase, and to this day I keep them in the garden of my heart.

****

Tears of Love

Looking out the window, I watch the rain fall.
It'll rain all day, getting wet everything in its reach. It's falling with more
power, the same power with which my heart won't stop crying for him.

Tears roll down my cheek and I can't control them.
They're tears of love, a love that's been lost for whatever reason.
A love that was divine, unequaled, exclusive.
A love that has left a void in my heart.

This void is so huge that my heart has not ceased to cry.
Ever since he left, I suffer with immense pain.

Tears of love;
they're the ones that I dry with the white handkerchief he himself gave to
me one day,
without knowing that it'd dry the tears of love that I shed for him.

Tears of love;
they're the ones that I cry.

Tears of love;
they're the ones that I need now, in order to forget him and end this
tragic chapter of my life.

****

The Angels

There is much to say about them, they are the best friends I have known in my life.

There are many kinds of them: playful, serious; elegant, athletic; painters, dancers, professors, doctors, chefs, etc.
There's such a tremendous variety of them; they come in all sizes, colors, and nationalities.

Hours will fly by talking about them. They are unconditional.
All you have to do is call them and they will come to you to be by your side, and they will do whatever possible to please you.

Our souls will be guided by them, if you ask it of them.
Dedicate time to them, they deserve it.
They also like to feel wanted and useful like us, human beings.

God knew perfectly well what he was doing when he made them, divine and celestial beings, the best messengers of the universe.

I have seen them, I have heard them, I have felt them. The sensation of peace that they have left me is something indescribable.
They are sublime.

Let's receive the gift God gave us and let's feel blessed by them.

We don't want to carry so much weight over ourselves.
Let's ask them to help us minimize our burden; they'd be happy to do so.

All you need to do is call them and you'll never be alone.

****

Fruits from the Orchard

Tomorrow I'll have to go to the orchard very early to pick the fruits
that you loved to eat for breakfast.

What days those were!
I remember them as if they were only yesterday.

But the most delightful thing of all was that we enjoyed it in every
aspect. We played, ran, and made Mom run after us.
We were always very close and very mischievous.

It was always like that until the day I parted.
I left in spring, leaving behind my family and my best sister, you.

I'm taking advantage of this opportunity that I found you and Mom on
my path to tell you both that I'm doing very well. If only you knew that I
still pick fruits from the orchard, still very early in the morning.

"Sister, don't be lazy and get up already! There's much to do.
Do you think that because I'm not there with you, you can do whatever
you want? Well, no! I'm watching you and you need to listen to Mom."

Don't worry about me, I know you always keep me in your thoughts,
the same way I keep you in my heart.
Always remember me with joy; it's the best way.

You'll make me very happy. Tomorrow, very early, I'll come so we
can go to the orchard, just like before - and don't tell Mom!

****

My Fairy Godmother

"I'd like to see my fairy godmother.
Ever since I was a child I had always heard that fairy godmothers visited
at night or day. It didn't matter how, I just wanted her to come now!"

I remember that my friends, Angela and Margaret, had seen their
fairy godmothers.
"It's amazing to see them," they told me.
"How come yours hasn't visited you yet?"

From that day on, I have always been curious to know her.
I was very excited and I asked myself, "What is she like?"

Those who had seen them described them as fat, skinny, tall, short;
the size didn't matter because they all had an angelic face.

I was anxious to see her, until one night in bed, ready to sleep and
reading my favorite book, I heard a soft voice, almost like a murmur.

I was between being awake and asleep, but I clearly heard
"Natalie, Natalie."
She called out my name! I quickly answered,
"Here I am, I can hear you.
Who is it who knows my name?"

"Your fairy godmother, the one you have always wanted to know."

I was left completely paralyzed. I couldn't believe it; after all these
years of waiting for her and she finally shows up now, right when I'm
about to get married!

She told me, "Age doesn't matter, nor does the time, nor do the
circumstances. We, the fairy godmothers, come to visit no matter how
old you are. All who believe in us should get to see their fairy
godmother, at least once in their lives.
We have that duty and we fulfill it with much love and dedication."

*"Today is the perfect day for me to present myself to you and to tell
you that my name is Quia.
I come from very far away, from a distant galaxy.*

*What's important is that I am here with you now.
I have come to wish you the greatest happiness of the world, and to tell
you that I'll be present on the day of your wedding.*

*Remember that I am your fairy godmother and that I have obligations
to fulfill, one of them being to accompany you on your special day. "*

*"From now on, whenever you need me, all you have to do is call me;
I'll come as quickly as possible. I'll come by plane if necessary. "
She leaned back and laughed.*

*She retired from my room and left behind a sensuous, delicate
fragrance; one of violets and roses.*

*She was of medium height, had blue eyes, red hair, and was very thin.
She wore a purple gown and purple shoes, with a lime green shawl and
a red neckerchief tied around her neck.
She was picturesque, striking, and very pretty.*

*But before she left she told me;
"I will light your way by lowering the stars of the universe to you.
I will give your life color by bringing the rainbow close to you,
and for your ears I will play the celestial harp. "*

What more can I ask for? She was fantastic!

Thank you for coming!

****

Christmas

A word so lovely that by simply being said it can bring us the most beautiful thoughts, memories, worries, joys, and all sorts of emotions, all with love.

One of the most beautiful times of the year, I personally think, is Christmas. It's like magic because it brings many changes in us all. It gives us the opportunity to celebrate the union of all who believe in Christmas, and it is a great celebration because the baby, Jesus, was born.

On this unequaled holiday let's do the impossible to reunite with our loved ones or friends. Our hearts fill with joy and our souls shine with a light that only Christmas can bring to them.

Children are those who wait for it the most, a holiday highly anticipated by all. It's time to love, forgive, please, and of course, give without expecting anything in return.

The nicest thing that Christmas brings us is the coming together of all who we love.
Even if they are far away, they are close in our thoughts and hearts.

Merry Christmas!

****

For You

May I always see your eyes looking at me, and have your sweet face to caress.

To feel your warmth, your laughter, your tears.

May I always see you walking barefoot, talking to the birds; how natural!

The way you are.

May I always see you run, jump, and dance.

May my eyes and my soul always see you smile.

May God protect you always.

For you, my doll, with all of my love.

-Mom

****

Thinking of You

May desperation and anguish never cloud you,
which often invade your soul.

Why grieve over things that are insignificant, next to the beautiful
things life brings you?

Waking up in the morning to see the sunlight coming in through your
window, greeting the new day with a smile, feeling full and grateful for
that extra day life gives you.

Come into contact with nature, observe it, take a walk in the fresh
air, hear the birds sing, and if it rains and we get wet, better yet,
for water is a great purifier.

Connecting with nature is connecting with God.

Life gives us so many lovely things; many times we don't see them,
because we don't want to.
And we have them so close and within our reach.

We need to learn how to observe and listen, because we're sensitive
beings, we have the ability to feel and perceive.

We would be able to fix all the problems of our soul if we only
listened to it more often.

Look inside yourself and you will see that you are great; great like
that ray of light that begins to enter your soul.
Now you can feel the joy of living life to the fullest.

Because that ray of light is the same God that is with you and will not
abandon you. You will always have him, just listen to your heart and you
will find him.

I only wanted to say that I was thinking of you today.

****

Forgiveness

Forgive me. I beg you from the bottom of my heart.
I will never do what I did again.

I know you suffered a great deal.
You felt like the world was ending and life was fading away from you.
Believe me, I never thought that the damage;
would have turned out to be so bad.

We are human beings; I don't want to excuse myself with this phrase
but only today, after everything that happened, I realize that we are able
to make those we love suffer.

I accept my mistake and I want you to accept my apology.

We will live more comfortably with our conscience,
otherwise we'd never be happy again.

Forgiveness is a process.
It isn't easy but neither is it impossible.

Forgive: a word that is often easy to pronounce but difficult to
accept, but you know that we grow as people if we forgive.

Making mistakes is human. We are here to make them, but we are
also here to learn to recognize them, as I am.

Now it's your turn to forgive and to follow the desires of your heart,
because I know you are a great person.

You haven't finished reading this letter and I already feel like you've
forgiven me. Wounds take time to heal but they do; that's where our
hearts will either come together or they will distance themselves in order
to follow their destiny.

****

Gemstone

I find you so beautiful with a unique shine.
Not only are you beautiful on the outside but even more so on the inside.

I'm sure when I say that I'm in love with a:
ruby, emerald, sapphire, aquamarine, topaz, turquoise, amethyst, etc.
Whatever its name, you are it.

You are like an angel sent down from heaven; a rainbow in all its
splendor; a night brightened by the stars; a vibrant sun that blinds me
with happiness; a green field with fresh grass
that's your beauty, so natural.

A spectacular jewel that can be beheld time and time again; one that
can't be stopped from being admired.

A gemstone.

One which I touch with silken hands to not leave any imprint of my
love; one to which I should say "I love you" only with my thoughts so
that I may not eclipse its radiance.

A gemstone is what I found and fell in love with.

A gemstone with the body and face of a woman, passionate and
totally sensual that shines with a light of her own.
That's how precious a woman you are.

****

<u>*Pleasure*</u>

What pleasure your gaze gives me,
to see those breathtaking eyes of yours.
It's as if they say to me,

"I love you."

What pleasure your lips give me,
that upon kissing me, the only thing I can feel is passionate magic.

What pleasure your hands give me,
that upon being touched I feel that you are driven crazy with love for me.

But the most pleasure I get is out of knowing that our hearts will
forever be unified in a magnificent place where our bodies and souls will
be complementary of each other in order to enjoy that pleasure which
only we are capable of feeling.

There are many pleasures in life,
but the greatest pleasure of all is undoubtedly that of love.

Oh, how big the feeling of love is!

Simply saying it produces a sensation of happiness inside us.

****

Positivity

"Daybreak, daybreak.
Who could always wake at daybreak?
Listen to the birds sing, look at a ray of light peeking in through the
window, feel the fresh breeze on my face.
A new day is born, and so is hope.
Daybreak, daybreak.
Who could always wake at daybreak?"

A little poem that came to my mind very early on a good day.
Where, without realizing it, my dream started to become reality.

And that is completely true - when I say "daybreak, daybreak" -
because we are waking up to a new day, another gift from this marvelous
life that God has given us, for us to enjoy it and take advantage of it
in a positive way.

And what are we supposed to do?
Change the way we think.
We are going through problems big and small that we all have, of all
shapes and colors.

But the attitude is what counts for everything - the positive attitude.
Get up in the morning and tell yourself,
"Yes, I can. I will not be beaten, I will get ahead.
Today is the day of my accomplishments, my triumphs, and my
opportunities."

And if everything you've planned for the day doesn't turn out the way
you wanted it to, remember that it's just one day, not every day of the
month. After all, we're imperfect beings.
We'll learn from this for the next time.
Be assured that life will give you the opportunity to succeed.

Positivity: a word that many people do not have as the very first in
their vocabulary.
It's a word so simple and helpful.

*Now, being positive doesn't mean that everything will turn out perfectly.
Remember that we are imperfect, and that's how we were created;
to try and perfect ourselves, nothing more.
Can you imagine a world full of perfect people?
How boring, right?*

*It's your attitude that will help you to face what could go wrong.
I would say that there lies the key to solving almost all of our problems.
It's so simple, all you have to do is change your attitude by thinking
positively.*

*Life in itself is already complicated and now in this day and age you
find difficulties everywhere, but it's there where you use your positivity
and at least you can see your problems from a different perspective.*

*You will notice that everything, absolutely everything has a solution,
some easier than others, but you will find them.*

****

Life is Beautiful

Wake up in the morning, see the birth of the day as if it were a flower opening its petals one by one.
It fills me with hope because I have twenty-four hours to be happy and I will take advantage of it!

To live one more day, filling it with joys, hopes, dreams for me to realize, goals for me to reach.

To enjoy a delectable dinner, to spoil myself - I deserve it!
To have a chat with a dear friend and share one another's joys and sorrows; to help those who need it, give company to those who feel lonely, hear them out and give them love.
There are so many ways one can give and receive love.

Your horizons will broaden; don't limit yourself.
Follow your instinct which is always alert.
Hear your inner voice, which is very wise, and you will find the directions that will take you to where you need to go.

To apologize for something you said accidentally.
Being the people that we are, we make mistakes, but we have the ability to recognize the good from the bad, and we will learn more each day.
Smile, and if you don't do it often. Learn.

If you think you don't have love, find it. It's up to you.
If you can't find it it's because you don't need it, because you already have love in your life.

To give or receive is the same, you have to have the feeling of doing so which is the motivator of your existence, which will serve as your daily nourishment.

I would write many more reasons why life is beautiful, but I think that what I've listed is enough; you should find out the rest for yourself and I'm sure you will figure it out.

"The biggest things become small and the smallest things become big."

****

Love Yourself

This letter is for all those who think they are on the bottom of the list.

I evidently do not think this way, but I ask them and I include myself out of sympathy:

What did we do today?

Did we worry about ourselves?

Did we love ourselves a little more?

Did we set new goals?

Did we buy that dress we liked to look at in the showcase in the store?

Did we set the table, put fresh flowers on it, and give it a nice tablecloth for ourselves?

Did we serve ourselves a glass of wine in the glasses that we usually use for guests?

Why do it for others when we can do it for ourselves?

So many questions all with the same answer.

From now on we are our own guests of honor.
That's how we should treat ourselves everyday, with attention, care, dedication and love for ourselves.

Because you are the protagonist of your life.

We made a list of all the people we need to or want to help, but you were left at the end. Helping our fellow man is important but helping ourselves is important as well.

We have a habit of leaving ourselves for last.

Why should we put ourselves at the end of the list?
Who will put us on the top of it?
Only ourselves.

Let's start with ourselves.
It's the only way we will be able to meet our goals in this life.
Nobody will come by and give you their place;
only you can give it to yourself.

It's time to change for our own good.
We should love ourselves more because we deserve to take pleasure in
the beautiful things there are on this equally beautiful planet.

Willpower is fundamental to all changes.
Our attitude should be positive, our priorities should shift.

Let's be happy with the wonders that God made available to all
human beings.
All we have to do is look for them to know that they are there.

If we love ourselves first, we'll be able to love our fellow man and
give everything we receive day after day.

Who will notice the change?
First we will and then those that we love.

I assure you that they will thank you for it!

****

My Dear

I want to tell you through these lines that I've always held you dear to me. I remember when we were children and everyone in the neighborhood thought that one day we would get married because they always saw us together. We didn't separate for anything.

What nice times those were. We grew up together and even believed that one day we would join together forever. We were so innocent.

The years went by and we moved away from each other for some reason or another. You went far away, you moved with your family to another city while I stayed in the town.

During our adolescence we still wrote to each other once in a while, until we came to the point where we knew nothing of each other.

I am a novice - a novice who will soon leave the Church.
I have always tried to serve God and I believe that I have done well, always fulfilling my obligations.

Today I realize that you are still in my heart, and I do not want to deceive to the Church as I have much respect for it, nor do I want to deceive myself.
I have decided to hang up the habit because I feel like it's something I should do. The truth should prevail before anything else.

I have no right to come into your life so suddenly, but I feel that I should at least tell you. I write to you so you will know what is going on with me and what my feelings are.
I know that you have not committed yourself to anyone and that you have not yet started a family.
I also know that you have always loved me as I love you.

Your sister, Victoria, came to the convent one day to visit with me and told me everything: that you're lonely and still in love with me. You've never forgotten about me.
I'm sure that we still have time to bind our lives together, look for me.

*You know where I live; in the same town and the same house where,
as children, we often played and as teenagers often tried to study but
ended up falling further in love.*

*I'll wait for you. I know you will come and we will unite our lives.
It is never too late for love. We will make our dreams reality.
I feel that our hearts will join together.*

*And we will love in the cabin,
the one we used to play in as children, remember?*

It was and will be our favorite place.

*The one, brightest star that always appeared in our romantic nights
whenever we dreamed of love will light up our lives and keep us
company. It has been and will continue to be our friend.*

My heart tells me that soon you will come to me.

****

Memories

I have many fond memories of you which are the ones that keep me alive. I bring to mind your infectious laughter, your youthfulness, your words of love, your good sense of humor and your whimsy, and all those feelings I have for you.

I can't hold back the tears when I think of you, whether they be of sadness or joy. That's my reaction toward you even though, for many moons, you have not been with me.

I remember when we climbed to the tops of the mountains, smelled the scent of fresh grass, and we sat at the summit and you told me; "Look at how small everything appears to be around us, but look at how big the sun is! My love for you is the same way."

You were always a dreamer, a lover of life, a mischievous child, a joker. You loved nature; when there was a full moon we went to the beach to sit down and admire it.
You said, "Look at how big the moon is!
My love for you is the same way."

I don't have you any longer, only the memories of you that I keep in the deepest part of my heart.

I will never forget you.

****

Reunion

I am waiting for you, counting the minutes, the hours, the days, the months. All this time has passed so quickly with the expectation of us meeting again and having our bodies come together, an indescribable passion that only you and I are familiar with, and which will flourish our love even more.

My heart races endlessly; I wait for you with much anxiety. I hope you like the place I have prepared with love for you.

All this time I've been sprucing up our little love nest. I want the best for us. I've added details that I am sure you will like, such as the fresh white flowers. Remember?

They were your favorite, you used to smell them every morning, and you said; "They have a delicious aroma, the same sensual kind that your body gives off when you wake up each morning."

You were always so thoughtful, loving and gallant.

You gave me everything, I did not need to ask you for a thing. I went as far as to think that you were a wizard - a wizard who was enchanting and in love, and one who could read my thoughts. You always knew ahead of time what I wanted or felt.

I am preparing an orange tart. Oh, how you loved oranges! I remember when we ran through the fields to pick oranges from the trees. You were always the first one there, and you yanked them off with great force and sank your teeth right into them.

And with the fresh juice running across your mouth, you kissed me with no intention of stopping, where we ended up lying on the grass. You had sensuality right on the surface. What times those were.

These are the moments of love that keep me standing with anticipation and hope. If I only told you that I am like I was back when I was fifteen, with many butterflies in my stomach.

Our reunion will be the best, you'll see.
You will not regret the step you are taking, there is nothing to fear.
Our love is very big and will overcome everything.

It's getting dark, the stars begin to shine in the sky and the moon
appears in all its glory.
It will be the sole witness of this passionate encounter.

Our bed will carry silk sheets, those in which our nude bodies will
find the harmony we need to go on the passionate journey that awaits us.

Finally! I can feel the awaited reunion approaching.

****

Easter Week

During these days of festivity, celebrating Easter Week, it's ideal for us to meditate, contact our inner self, and discover feelings that have been hidden and we have not had the time to bring them to the surface.

We should take advantage of these days of contemplation to the maximum. There are many people who use Easter Week as an excuse to go out on vacation to break the routine of daily life.

But I also think it's the perfect time to pay attention to our spiritual side the way we do with our body and mind.

Today, people talk a lot about the spirituality that we all keep within ourselves, and for different reasons we haven't made it as important as it deserves to be. Well, now is the time to do it.

Can you imagine if much of the world put it in practice? I don't want to be too optimistic by thinking this way, which would be too much to ask, but I think it would be something wonderful.

We would be able to live better, in every sense of the word, in this marvelous world God has gifted us and that we, human beings, have not cared for it the way it ought to be. As a result we start to complain about all the misfortunes, that affect our environment.

The angels and the energies of the universe are waiting for you to come into contact with them, for you to tell them your troubles, worries, joys, plans; in short, everything you want.

They will be of great help; you will not feel alone. There is no reason to be, having divine beings around us, and if you can not feel them, call them.

They will be glad to help you and give you spiritual support.

For this reason let us take advantage of the days of Easter Week and ask for whatever we desire.

Families will gather to celebrate the resurrection of Jesus, son of God, who returns to save the humanity that needs it now more than ever.

What better time for meditation and communication.

Have an excellent Easter Week!

****

There is Always Something to Learn

"Would you care to dance?"
"Yes, I'd love to."

That's how our love started, since that day we danced so closely that
we would never separate.

It was a path full of flowers, like the ones that you gave me.
How happy we were, everything seemed rosy to us.

It was love, that word so big and wonderful.
I had no idea that you could get so much with it.

But over time our love changed. It was different. I would say that it
was a more mature love with experiences of all kinds, good and bad.
But it had to go through everything for us to move forward as a couple.

We grew together, since we were so young back then.
Learning was what we needed to do. "Get ahead," a complicated phrase.
How does one learn to get ahead?

Who teaches us the secrets of life?
No one! Absolutely no one!
We do it by falling down on a daily basis and getting back up just the
same. But that's the life of all humans - we were created to learn.

We raised our children with all of our love and we taught them the
values which they hold onto to this day, which serve as the pillars of
their lives: respect, appreciation, and above all, love, which is the most
important thing in the world.

I think we've done the most that we could, always with effort.
Nothing is free and there is always something to pay.
That is how one learns to live.

And at this stage in life there remains only the two of us, and I ask myself, "Is there something else for us to learn?

*Yes, now we have to learn how to live on our own.
Life is a constant lesson, and learning I the only way to live and be happy."*

*And you would ask me, "Shall we dance?"
And I would say, "Of course!"*

We still have all the time in the world, now that there are just the two of us; just like when we boarded the train of love and decided to start our own story; just you and me.

It's time to get off at the next station.

To take a long walk being happy and looking forward, and if we turn and look back we will feel that we have done everything, we could have and wanted to.

Complete satisfaction.

*We walk hand in hand, remembering how happy we were.
Today and forever.*

****

Loneliness

I feel immense sadness when I look at your portrait and I can't see you around me. I hear my soul grieve and I feel my body fading.

What happened to us after all the love that we shared?

What happened in our lives?
Was it that sadness came to my door,
let itself in without my noticing and stayed?

I want to think that this is just a nightmare, a bad dream and soon I will wake up.

I will always value your time with me, but now that you're not here I can't resist it. I'm weak and I fear loneliness.
I don't think there is any human being on earth,
who is not afraid of being alone.

I have loved you so very much that I have no more love to give.
I'm like a wilting flower,
dying of thirst from being unable to drink the elixir of your kisses.

You took my heart, my will to live, and my happiness for all time.
Now I only have misery, sorrow, and melancholy.

Three emotions that intend to stay with me, but who I want to keep far, far away from me.

The loneliness I feel has left a deep impression in my heart and soul;
one that will be difficult to erase.

****

Sigh of Love

I sigh for you, I sigh for them and also for myself.

I sigh for the present, the past - which has gone - and the future;
what will it bring?

There is much to sigh about, but the biggest sigh I have to give is for
all of you.

For those I love and all the love I receive everyday.
Love that is good, clean, and pure.

I will continue sighing as long as I live.

And when I die, I will continue sighing.

Now I say goodbye, but not without giving one more sigh.
It won't be the last.

A sigh of love is what I have in my heart for you.

****

Cup of Tea

What a rich aroma that came out of my kitchen!
It could only be the delicious tea of mixed essences which I was about to
drink, when suddenly you appeared in my thoughts!

To my mind came one memory after another.
Those of our long conversations, moments of love; of friendship, of
cooperation, and of madness.
I would say we had so much enjoyment that we lost track of time.

I remember it like it was yesterday, when you'd ask me for a cup of
tea. I prepared it for you with so much love that you'd ask me,

"What did you put into this tea that makes it so delicious?"
I replied, "Only love."
It was our moment of peace and tranquility.

We made a thousand plans and traveled with our imagination to
places we could only dream of.
We could have been talking about us, until the scent of that delicious tea
had started to disappear, which indicated that both the tea and our
meeting were coming to an end.

I think of the beautiful moments we spent together,
and to think it all started with a cup of tea.

I am about to have a drink,
except that this time you are not here with me to enjoy it.

But I am sure that our thoughts will,
because the aroma of the tea I am drinking will reach you.

And I will be waiting; with a cup of tea.

****

I Miss You, My Love

*I miss that time that was the best for me, full of mystery which we
used to see each other and bring to the surface all that love that we had.*

*Your love for me was delirious.
I came to think that it was all an illusion,
where I didn't want to see reality.
But it was so real, the way we were loving each other.*

*I miss your caresses, your fiery kisses, your body wet with salt water,
and the moments of silence where there was no need to speak,
where nothing more was needed except the two of us, forever in love.*

*I didn't understand how one could miss something so immensely.
There were moments I ran out of air;
you had become my oxygen and my will.*

*The days go by with no meaning to me; the nights are long and
endless. Without you my life will never be the same.*

*My body feels cold. You're not here anymore to give me the heat of
your love, a love without equal, which lit up and grew each day, turning
into a kind of passion that was indescribably irrational.*

I miss you, my love.

****

Your Lover

I am your lover, and what's wrong with that?
Maybe everything or nothing.
I'm sorry to say this, but those few hours you spend with me mean a lot
to me. They are hours stolen for love.

I don't know if you are committed and I don't want to know.
All I know is that I met you on a very rainy and cold day, and upon
looking at you I felt a warmth that ran throughout my body,
transforming the cold of winter into true passion.

I love you dearly; you have driven me crazy with love.
Perhaps I'm being selfish, and I don't think of anyone else,
but I love you and I will be your lover for as long as you want.

That's how much I'm in love;
I will conform and I will not demand anything of you.

Love is not bought nor begged for, but if I had to do that and more
for you, I would without giving it any thought.

Your warmth, your kisses, your caresses, the way you love;
it all has made me your slave.

You bring out in me a passion that's indescribable and subliminal.

Is there a specific time to love and to choose the right person?
No, there isn't. Is it love that chooses us?

Love comes and takes possession of our heart, invading all of our
senses and emotions, leaving us helpless and occupying every inch of
our body, soul, and mind.

All I know is that destiny has prepared this wonderful encounter for
us and I would not want it to ever end.

Who can go against destiny?

It has everything ready and it can do what it wants with us.
We are cardboard puppets to it, and it brings us together and separates
us when we least expect it.

Today we have to go through this test of love and we would not like to
be judged. So, my love, let's not waste any more time.
The clock is already ticking and you know that time is our first enemy.

****

Smile

You once told me,
"You have a lovely smile."
Ever since that day, I lost my mind over you.
I don't know what happened to me, but I fell in love.

Love at first sight or love at the first smile?

But you too lost your mind over me.
You fell in love like a teenager.
We were both madly in love, hanging onto a cloud of white cotton.

Those were such nice times. We ended up knowing each other so well
that it was like we were made for each other.
We had the same likes and we even fought at the same time!

You always used to say:
"Never lose that beautiful smile that I fell for. It's angelic and sensual.
You know that with a smile you can find everything.
You have me in your hands, crazy out of love for you."

Life went on and we were happier than ever,
spending our whole day with each other.

Today, I no longer smile; that beautiful love has gone forever.

Where is he? With whom is he spending his days and nights?
To whom is he giving his love?

Sadness has taken me over and I don't think I can go back to smiling
the way I used to.

He left taking my love and my smile.

****

A Friend That Was

*After some time of not seeing you, you have changed; a lot or a little,
I don't know. I don't recognize you. I have changed too.
It's human nature to go through changes.
Maybe one day it was a nice friendship, but now it isn't anymore.*

*Life has brought us together again and as much as I try to get close
to you, there is something that prevents me from doing so.
It's not easy to say this but I must.
My conscience will be at ease to know that I speak the truth.*

*Why seek an explanation for everything?
We want to investigate the farthest depths when the simplest answer is in
front of us. We have almost nothing in common.*

*We think differently. I think we are different; today I realize that we
always were. Now is the time to say goodbye and not try to understand
the incomprehensible any further.
Our friendship was nice while it lasted.*

*Many things separate us which I will not dare to list - thousands of
reasons, you with your ideas and I with mine.
I don't like to judge anyone.
We are free to be and think whatever we want, respecting each other.
The best thing to do is to end this chapter of our lives here and now.*

*I will keep the best memories of our friendship.
It's not bad to be incompatible but neither is it good.*

*It is best for each of us to go our own way, and if we ever meet up
again, we will greet each other, ask about each other's lives,
and continue on our own course.*

*Just as life has brought us together one day,
so will it separate us today.*

I wish you the best of this world. Good luck.

****

An Uninvited Friend

I will introduce to you a friend who I'm sure you know very well.

She is never invited, but...

I have felt her close, very close.
I even thought that she had been living with me for a long time.
I have tried to ignore her but with no success.
She insists on staying and the worst of it all is that many times,
she actually does.

I think that she is looking for someone to spend her short stay with.
I'm sure she feels lonely and wants company.
I've asked her,
"How can something like this happen to you? Just you?"

"People try to avoid me, thinking I'm bad company, but that's not how
it is. What they don't know is that I am neither good nor bad company;
I am necessary and everyone needs me at some point in their lives even
though they often try to ignore me."

I wondered what I could do to get her away from my side,
if one day she appeared.

One day without realizing it, I entered her life and she so subtly
accommodated to mine. I remember that on many occasions and
different circumstances, in the tranquility of my home, I felt her arrive.

But who could it be that I am speaking of so casually?

Her name is Loneliness. Do you know her?
Has she visited you once and wanted to stay?
Well, she looks for company, too; incredible! But it's that simple.
She is also alone!

Loneliness goes on her way and comes in through the front door.
She gets comfortable in your senses, your mind, and your heart, and
without you noticing she becomes your companion.

On second thought, it isn't a bad idea to have her as a friend.
When you don't want to talk to anyone, she'll be there to listen to your
complaints and your joys in silence.
A silence which sometimes seems endless.

Loneliness will go when she needs to, and if we need her she will
come, like a loyal friend.

The truth is, we've become very good friends.
We often don't ask or demand each other for anything.
I leave her her space and she leaves me my own.

Even though it seems a little absurd, we need her more than we think.
She helps us make decisions, think, dream, heal heartaches and more.

Loneliness, the uninvited friend: now she has an invitation!

****

A Letter From Heaven

It's too early - five in the morning. Time for me to go.
Don't cry Mom, Dad - it's the first thing I think about when I feel my
heart beat very slowly, almost without strength.

The time for me to pass on has come; to see the other side even
though my guardian angels, as I call them, have prepared me for this
moment. They have been coming very frequently lately to accompany me
as I meet with those who have gone before me.
I am calm because I know where I am going.

I will tell you a little about where I find myself before leaving this
sore body and giving my last breath.

I saw them arrive, about four of them, and they all brought an
amazing peace. The same kind of peace I felt at the moment of my
departure. I could easily feel the great love they had for me.
They came into my room, smiling at me so sweetly
and I smiled at them in return.

They said to me;
"You will go with us, we will make the trip together. You will never be
alone. Don't be afraid. We will be your guides, today and forever, as
long as you need us. We love you too much to leave you alone."

And that's how it went. The light they had brought was so strong that
it blinded me slightly, but I could still see them.
I heard a chorus around me, one of angels, with melodious, celestial
voices that made me feel so good, that without realizing it, I already
started to cross into the spiritual realm.

By leaving this world, the material world, where I was happy, where I
was fulfilling my goals, I was also leaving my parents who I know will
not have comfort until they read this letter.

I was leaving behind dear friends, my material things, and all of my
earthly pleasures; eating, dancing, shopping, etc.

At one point I thought, "Where are they taking me?"
But the peace I felt was so big that I let myself be carried away by them.
Thus I crossed once and for all into the spiritual world, where I found
nothing more and nothing less of a paradise, where there was no pain,
anxiety, or fear; only peace and love in abundance.

I wanted to know everything at once but they told me to be patient,
for I had all the time in the world to learn.
I was anxious to discover everything.
"What was it like? What was on the other side?"
But I realized I had to wait.

They asked me;
"Have you noticed that you have died in the physical world?
That you will no longer live among your loved ones in the same way?"

"In what way?"
"In the terrestrial way.
Now you will do so from here, the spiritual world."

What that meant was:
"You can see them, your family and friends,
but you won't be able to touch them.
There will be other ways of communication that you will slowly learn
about. You'll see."

At that moment I felt intense misery and I burst into tears.
One of them hugged me and whispered, "Don't be sad.
From here you will always be with them.
You will never leave them, and the moment they need you, you will go to
them; and rest assured that they will know, because in some way you will
manifest."

I see my parents grieving brokenheartedly.
I should be there to console them, to tell them that I am fine here and
that I love each and every one of them.

"How do I do it?"
I ask myself anxiously, wanting to learn everything fast.
At that moment, one of my guides with the most tender look on its face
told me, "This is your opportunity to communicate with them."

"How will I?" I ask it.
"Close your eyes and enter their hearts.
Tell them how well you're doing here."

I closed my eyes and thought of them with so much love, that I felt
they could sense me. I saw them both together.
Mom and Dad, say to one another, "We feel you, sweetie. We feel you."
At that moment I realized that what I had been told about
communication had been absolutely true.

I felt relaxed. I could see how my body was placed in a coffin, where
it would be kept day and night.

From that place called "Beyond,"
I could see the entire funeral, friends and family included.
Everyone was very sad with my passing and remembered me
with much fondness.

But the best thing of this all was that I could communicate by means
of the mind and heart, and I told my parents;
"This place is very nice! I can do everything and I don't feel pain!"

Then, I saw my mother smile, despite the pain she felt for my
departure, shaking her head the way somebody says,
"What are you talking about?"

That's how our spiritual conversation continued, trying to give peace
and comfort, something that will take a long time to come when there is
such a large wound in the heart.

A few school friends of mine arrived and I played a joke on them.
As they approached the coffin, I untied one of the shoelaces of the new
shoes that had been put on me. They were surprised!

I don't know why we need to be so neatly dressed and have everything
in its place on the day of our funeral.
We're already dead and how we look on the outside isn't important
anymore. What matters is how your soul and spirit are.
To me, everything was run well.

Continuing with the shoelace trick, there was only one shoe with its
lace untied, and my schoolmates called my mom to fix it.
She did so, and she knew it was a sign.
I was very mischievous; all of my friends knew that I was the joker of the
class. But she didn't understand it - yet.

This wonderful letter is for you, my dear family, to explain to you a
bit more how we communicate with our loved ones.
That was a sign that I sent to my school friends,
telling them that I was fine.

I tell you all this so you know that death is not bad; we never die
completely. We can still see those that we love most and they will be
happy to know that we can communicate with each other no matter
where we are.

I was with you on the day of the funeral and I know I was felt.
I was never alone.
They, my angels and spirit guides, were with me the whole time.

I know this letter will give you much peace because I heard you
silently say; "What were the last minutes of our adored child like?"
Don't worry anymore, I was always with God.

I visit you on birthdays, anniversaries, and births.
Now you're grandparents and I have two beautiful nieces, daughters of
my younger sister. Things are happening and I am finding out about
everything. I will always be with you.

Many years have passed and I am still here - I haven't gone anywhere.

By the way, I've had the joy of receiving one of my grandparents and he
is the same as always.
He doesn't look a day older since I last saw him.

He has already reunited with me and you don't know how well we're
doing. He has a great sense of humor and always makes us laugh.

Here, no one measures time, simply because time doesn't exist.
A minute can be a year and a year, a minute.
The only things that exist are us, the spirits, who arrive to stay until we
are needed to go back again.

"Will we be reincarnated?"
If so, I'd like to be a painter, an artist.
I've always liked painting but I didn't have the time necessary to do so.
It looks like here I will have a lot of free time.
And I should take advantage of it.

For now I will continue learning more and more.
For the moment I am well. I am prepared to keep greeting those whose
turn it is to pass on and leave their physical body to become a spirit.
Now I can say that we do not die entirely.

To all those who have lost a loved one: there is no need to be sad
because we, the spirits, sense all types of emotions and if you become
depressed, we will be too.

I am doing well and I want to tell you that we will always
communicate.
What we have here, in my new home, is a lot of love to give and receive.

From the depths of my soul, I love all of you and I miss you as well.
"How couldn't it be that way?"

I want to see you happy, otherwise I'll get sad.
"Who wants to see a sad soul?" Nobody!

I've met all kinds of people, well, souls, I mean; a bit of everything.
By talking with them I have learned so much.
I spend what feels like hours talking with doctors, professors, painters,
writers, athletes, artists and so much more.

I met a girl who died of cancer.
She's nice, her soul is as clean and pure as spring water.
I could talk to her all the time.

Now I better understand my spiritual guides.
Now I understand why they are so happy.
What there is here is wonderful

But there is not always something that can be fixed.
However, everything has a solution, and how!
Problems are solved very quickly and especially with much love.

Coexistence is fantastic!

It's time for me to go. I'll write to you soon, or I will visit you,
whichever you prefer.

Until next time, family!

****

A Night in Siena

*Sofia and I had decided to go on vacation to the wonderful
Mediterranean country Italy.
We wanted to spend two weeks differently.
We'd be going to the beautiful city of Siena,
situated in the region of Tuscany.*

*We loved the green meadows of the region.
The fresh air that we breathed was ideal for relaxing and
communicating with our inner selves, which was something that we
really needed to do.*

*We felt the necessity to retreat to that city and we had to follow our
intuition. Sofia is very sensitive and has always been such in a lot of
things. She is one of those who, as they say, have their sixth sense well
developed. So do I. You already know what I'm talking about.*

*I remember the day before while we talked about where we wanted to
go, we looked into each other's eyes and said, "Italy!"*

*The house we rented was amazing.
It was very well-located on the top of a hill with a breathtaking view.
The two of us sitting at the top, we could easily see the city of Siena.
"There is no view more beautiful than this in the world," I thought.*

*Night was approaching fast. What would it bring?
Not every night is the same in Siena.
They all have their unique charm.*

*I watched the sky intently, as if waiting for the stars to appear one by
one, of all sizes, shining they way only they can,
with a light of their own.*

*Sitting in the garden of our house at the foot of the hill with clear
skies above, we could see all of the stars hovering in the sky.
We couldn't get enough of looking at them, but suddenly we both
shouted,
"I saw you! I saw you! Who are you?"*

Soon after, we heard a whisper that said:
"Are you Sofia and Martha?" They asked about us!
We were so excited that we got goose bumps. They came from the stars.

"We will brighten your lives, we will give peace and love to your
souls. Don't be afraid, we are angels of light," they told us.
We were obviously speechless.

We had the feeling that something wonderful would happen to us that
night, and we were not mistaken.
Sofia and I looked into each other's eyes and we thought:
"I think we'd love to keep dreaming."
But it wasn't a dream; it was reality!

The next morning, we woke up very peacefully.
We were sure that it wasn't a dream.
What had happened the night before was, without a doubt, that we had
been visited by "them."
Now we understood why we had to be in such a special place.

"They" had everything planned for us.
Ever since that night our lives changed and our hearts never felt lonely
again. We could be certain that we knew the true and unconditional love
that only "they" could give.

****

Seeing You Again

My heart became excited with happiness when I saw you again.
We talked and I understood that it wasn't bad to be there.
Now I can understand you better.

You looked so happy that it was contagious, and I caught it from you.
You are at peace. I can feel your smile and your heartbeat.
It was so lovely for us to meet. You've hardly changed at all.
To me, you are the same as when you left.

We recalled old times, but we did so with joy. We all have to go.
You were too young when you left. You just started to live, and that made
me sad. You raised your baby from heaven, you protected and guided it,
and you will continue to do so.

Everyday you visit your child. You give yourself the time for it, like
all mothers do with their children. I've seen you take it into your arms,
sing to it and also cry.

It was nice to see each other. I know we will do it again.
When you feel lonely and want to talk a little, you can count on me
because I will be there to hear you out like I always have.
You know how to reach me.

I know that I will see you again.

****

Wrong Flight

It's ten o'clock in the morning and I must hurry since I need to go to the
airport to pick him up. I haven't seen him for five years.
His flight will arrive at noon. I'll take a shower and then get dressed so I
can be as pretty as I can.

I should impress him. I can't believe that I will see him soon.
My heart is pounding a mile a minute; I am so nervous, as when I was
fifteen and I secretly met up with my boyfriend.

I remember when he left and I went to say goodbye.
I never imagined that he'd be away for so long.

We've written each other so many letters that I had enough to write a
book; a book about love. There was so much love in those words that
sometimes I came to think that he was here with me.
I could even feel his warmth and kisses.

Will he feel the same way about me as he did the first time we met?
What will he think of me?
I was so nervous that I had many questions,
but none came with an answer.

I better hurry up; I'd like to see him arrive through the corridor,
then I'll run up and give him a great big hug.
I already feel butterflies in my stomach.

I finished with my shower and then got dressed.
I chose to wear the best dress, a red one which happened to be my
favorite color. I've only used it for special occasions and this was indeed
a very special one! To tell the truth, I haven't worn it before, so this
would be its debut. What better reason than this?

I don't mean to brag, but, once I finished dressing up I looked
spectacular. There was no doubt that I wanted to impress him and that's
exactly how it would be.

I called a taxi which came almost immediately.
It took me straight to the airport, and while I was on my way, I thought
about everything we had lived through.

*I recalled how we were always in love, the nights of love and the
moments of passion we spent together.
I don't think he could have forgotten either.*

*Between thoughts, the taxi arrived at the airport.
I never had so many mixed emotions. I really should be relaxed;
I don't want to spoil this special moment - a moment of love,
exclusive and long-awaited.*

*I approach the counter and anxiously ask for flight number 1550 and
was told that the flight had already come in and the passengers were
about to disembark the plane.*

*My legs were shaking; the butterflies took control of not only my
stomach but the rest of my body, but I had to be calm.
I waited for an hour and he did not appear.*

*I started to worry. Could it be that he became discouraged at the last
minute? Did something happen to him?
My god, I think I'm going to faint; I'm starting to run out of air.
Why isn't he here?
A thousand thoughts were going through my head.*

*Already uneasy, I approach the counter a second time, give his full
name, and after five minutes they tell me;
"The person you are waiting for is not on the list of passengers.
You have the wrong flight."*

*In that moment, I felt relieved. I was already imagining the worst and I
nearly had a nervous breakdown.*

*From being so anxious to see him I thought that today was the day of his
arrival, plus I had the wrong flight, too!
Feeling more relaxed, I went back home.*

*"Marsha, wake up, wake up! What flight are you talking about?"
my mother asks me. "Wake up or you'll be late for work."*

I woke up and happily realize that it was all a dream.

*I don't know what I would have done if it had been true.
I would have died from grief from
waiting and waiting and not seeing him appear.*

*The phone rang, I answered and I heard his voice on the other line say;
"My love, I have to travel tomorrow for two weeks.
Would you take me to the airport?"
I was so shocked that I couldn't answer.*

*Immediately I ask, "How long will you be gone?"
"Two weeks," he told me.
I then asked, "What's your flight?"
"1731."
Upon hearing his reply I become calm.*

*Then I understood that everything had been a dream and I could breath
easy. That definitely wasn't the number of the flight, the one which I
waited for that afternoon because he never embarked in the first place.*

*He never left my side. I remember he canceled the trip for the future, and
from that day on I loved him even more. I realized that I loved him so
much that my life wouldn't be the same without him.*

*It was a dream, but with a message of love. It made me think that many
times we value those who we have beside us when we feel we will lose
them or, in the worst case, have already lost them.*

*We went on a trip together, where love and passion were the guests of
honor. And, just in case, I always travel with him.*

****

Ballet Slippers

How beautiful she looked with her ballet slippers and her white dress. She looked like a princess sent down from the heavens, and she danced like an angel, a celestial goddess.

Her skin was delicate, like porcelain, and she had a slim figure. She looked so fragile, it almost seemed like she would break.

I came almost daily just to see her dance. She didn't look like she ever got tired. She had so much vitality, always spinning on her tiptoes. She was like a ballerina in a music box.

Until one afternoon I waited for her to come onto the dance floor, like she always did. I waited for several hours, only this time she didn't appear.

I asked for her and they told me, "It's been a while since we last saw her. We miss her, especially her sensual dancing. We believe she has gone to live in another city. We won't be seeing her again either. She was beautiful, an exceptional, unique dancer. We never knew where she came from and now we don't know, where she is."

A few years had passed and I decided to return to the place where she danced, to remember her. She left a mark on me - a mark of love. A love that was silent and hidden.

I never had the opportunity to tell her. If only I could see her again for one minute, then I would tell her that I loved her very much; that her dancing and natural beauty captivated me; that she brought light into my life.

I decided to sit in front of the dance floor with the illusion of seeing her, putting my hopes in that empty floor, that was more lonely now than ever.

Suddenly the whole room lit up and she appeared.
She had returned!
She started dancing and I couldn't believe it.
We were both there, alone.
She was so lovely, like a crystal doll, with a natural shine.

She kept looking at me.
It was love. It could only be love.

She smiled at me and my heart fluttered with joy.
I told her that I loved her and I loved her dancing as well.
She looked at me and said; "I love you, too."
Those were her final words.

Everything ended. I don't know at what moment she finished dancing.
I couldn't see her anywhere. She disappeared right in front of my eyes!
I was frozen, totally surprised.

With a heavy heart, I walked toward the exit, when I spot on the small
table in the entrance hall her ballet slippers.
She left them for me - they had to be just for me.
She had given them to me as a gift!

I felt so much joy that I took them with me and I protected them like
treasure. I put them in a glass case on the mantel of my chimney where I
could admire them every day of my life.

The golden ballet slippers belonged to a ballerina who came from a
very far place to stay, but a fatal disease took her life at an awfully
young age. Just when she was beginning to know love.

But her indescribable beauty and my love for her had stayed with me,
and I carry her etched in my heart. She was the same person I had
watched dance for all these years. She was gone forever, leaving me her
most prized possession, her ballet slippers.

****

The Traveler

I've always known that sailors have many loves, so many that they can
hardly count them all.
Something like: a girl in every port.
Could that be true, or are those just stories that people have made up?
What could be the truth? I'll never know.

What I do know for sure is that my sailor only has me.
I don't want to sound conceited, but I am sure that I am the only one.
He visits many ports, but he only stops at mine. He doesn't come very
often, but when he does he only belongs to me and I to him.

Traveler with a wandering soul.

Our love is so grand that when we get together everything feels like a
fantasy. We take advantage of each moment and treat it like it's the last.
He is so in love with me.

He comes to visit me once a month, but that one moment in time turns
into many nights of pleasure, desire, passion, lust; our love is so great
that our senses rise to a level of delirium
a delirium that often provokes us to love madly.

My beloved traveler,
I wait for you, don't delay.
You will always have me and I will always have you.

At least that's what I think. Don't ever deceive me.
Deceit in love is the most painful thing. The wounds that it would leave
would be as big as the love that I feel for you.
The wounds of love are the ones that take the longest to close.

Traveler with a wandering soul.

I'm writing this to you because you are taking longer than you should.
Why are you taking so long to come? I'm waiting for you so anxiously.
I won't worry anymore. I know you'll come soon.

I can't live without you, the way you can't live without me, without my caresses and all the love I give you night after night.

Traveler, how much longer will you keep visiting?
How much longer will you keep giving me pleasure?
How much longer will we continue to love each other?

I don't know.

I know that you will come; at any moment I will feel your footsteps.

You will open the door with the only key that you have
the key of passion is the only one that will open my heart.

****

A Letter For You

"Who hasn't read and written a letter in their life?"
I'm sure all of us have done it. Letters of love, farewells, joy, greetings,
good wishes and even bad, intrigue, suspicion, sadness, etc.

The page wouldn't be big enough for me to list the reasons and motives
there are to write letters. But the most important reason is to
communicate, to let out all the emotions we have inside our heart and
soul. I am sure that in this marvelous book, you have found a special
letter for you.

For many years humans have used different forms of written
communication, whether it be symbols, hieroglyphs, letters, etc.
Everything is valid for communicating, using all methods to make
yourself understood.

They're written in stone, fabric, metals; an infinite amount of various
materials, including paper, which is one medium that is best known by
all of us. And with the introduction of the Digital Age, we now use the
Internet as well. Any medium is valid for good communication.
We will always continue writing and reading.

For those who at some point in their lives received letters, they kept them with the idea of going back to read them but have forgotten about them for a while. Naturally, they will be found deteriorated, the paper of a different color, and will go to waste.

But to keep on hand a book of letters is something different,
it's to read them whenever and wherever you want.
If by reading "Each From The Heart; Special Letters Just For You"
you felt that in some way you could identify with them,
this book would have fulfilled its duty: to reach the souls, hearts, and minds of the people.

Thank you and good luck to all.
Maria Manuela Pinto

ABOUT THE AUTHOR

Maria Manuela Pinto lives in the United States, in the sunshine state of Florida. She likes to socialize and keep in touch with people. She thinks that communication is key. Any kind of communication is essential in every stage of a human being's life. Surrounded by art for most of her life, this in turn influenced her decision to write and has helped her to channel her thoughts. *Each from the Heart: Special Letters Just For You* expresses love, a divine sentiment, and it is the protagonist of this marvelous book.

www.mariamanuelapinto.com
facebook.com/MariaManuelaPintoAuthor
twitter.com/MariaManuelaPi4

Publisher: Mariangelikuss

Mariangelikuss